The Rocky Mountain Fur Trade

James P. Burger

The Rosen Publishing Group's
PowerKids Press™
New York

For Richard "Ski" Konzielaski, who conquered the Rockies with practiced ease

Published in 2002 by The Rosen Publishing Group, Inc.
29 East 21st Street, New York, NY 10010

First Edition

Book Design: Emily Muschinske

Project Editor: Kathy Campbell

Photo Credits: pp. 5 (reenactment and mountains), 6 (bear, fox, beaver, otter), 21 (fox pelts) © National Geographic; pp. 5 (mountain man holding pelt), 10 (trekkers), 12, 14 (top hat man) © Archive Photos; pp. 6 (mountains), 17 (Jim Bridger), 18 (buckskin man) © Jim Winkley/CORBIS; pp. 8, 9, 10 (mountain man), 13, 14 (beavers), 17 (boat), 18 (dandy man) © The Granger Collection, New York; p. 21 © N. Carter/North Wind Picture Archives.

Burger, James P.
  The Rocky Mountain fur trade / James P. Burger.— 1st ed.
    p. cm. — (The library of the westward expansion)
  Includes index.
    ISBN 0–8239–5851–5 (library binding : alk. paper)
  1. West (U.S.)—History—To 1848—Juvenile literature. 2. Rocky Mountains—History—19th century—Juvenile literature. 3. United States—Territorial expansion—Juvenile literature. 4. Fur traders—West (U.S.)—History—19th century—Juvenile literature. 5. Pioneers—West (U.S.)—History—19th century—Juvenile literature. 6. Trappers—West (U.S.)—History—19th century—Juvenile literature. 7. Fur trade—West (U.S.)—History—19th century—Juvenile literature. 8. Frontier and pioneer life—West (U.S.)—Juvenile literature. [1. West (U.S.)—History—To 1848. 2. Rocky Mountains—History—19th century. 3. United States—Territorial expansion. 4. Fur traders. 5. Pioneers. 6. Trappers. 7. Fur trade. 8. Frontier and pioneer life.] I. Title.
  F592 .B95 2002
  978'.02—dc21

                                                                                            00–012924

Manufactured in the United States of America

Contents

1 North American Fur   4

2 A Fresh Place to Hunt   7

3 John Jacob Astor   8

4 Ashley and Henry   11

5 Rendezvous   12

6 Beaver Traps   15

7 Famous Mountain Men   16

8 The Mountain Men's Success   19

9 Killing Wildlife   20

10 The Last Rendezvous   22

Glossary   23

Index   24

Web Sites   24

North American Fur

Millions of **fur-bearing** animals once lived in the North American wilderness. During the 1600s and 1700s, French and English fur companies built forts around the Great Lakes and in the Ohio River Valley. Large hunting parties and many Native Americans trapped in the wilderness. Then they brought their furs to these companies' forts to sell or to trade for **manufactured goods**.

Fox, bear, otter, and especially beaver were the most popular animals to hunt. Trappers wanted them for their pelts, which were the animals' skins with the fur still attached. Pelts were very popular because they were used for making hats, coats, and other types of clothing. People continued to trap until it seemed that few animals were left in the region of the Great Lakes and the Ohio River Valley.

Left: *A fur trapper carries a metal trap and an animal's pelt.*

Bottom: *This man is dressed as a fur trapper. He is taking part in an event in Pinedale, Wyoming. This event honors trappers every July and is called The Green River Rendezvous.*

Red Fox

Black Bear

Beaver

Otter

A Fresh Place to Hunt

After the American Revolution (1775–83), the United States grew quickly as a country. President Thomas Jefferson bought the Louisiana **Territory** from France in 1803. The explorers Meriwether Lewis and William Clark took a voyage to map this large area of land west of the Mississippi River. When Lewis and Clark returned from their two-year trip, they reported that fur-bearing animals lived all over the **Far West**. There were few fur-bearing animals left where early hunters had trapped. Some people still hoped to become rich by selling furs, though. Lewis and Clark's reports made these people consider going farther west for a fresh place to trap.

After Lewis and Clark's voyage, fur trappers began to hunt in western areas for such fur-bearing animals as these. The Rocky Mountains (seen at left) became a popular area for fur trade companies.

DID YOU KNOW?

Lewis and Clark did more than make maps of the areas they explored. President Jefferson asked them also to take careful notes about the plants, animals, and Native Americans they met along the way.

John Jacob Astor

An American named John Jacob Astor formed the American Fur Company in 1808. He first tried fur trading in the Ohio River Valley but found it too hard and the animals too **scarce** to make much money. In 1810, Astor sent some men to Oregon and instructed them to set up a fur-trading fort there. Astor's new company, called the Pacific Fur Company, did not last long either. When the War of 1812 broke out between the United States and Great Britain, fur trading in the Pacific Northwest, which is Oregon and Washington today, became dangerous. British soldiers soon claimed Astor's new fort, Fort Astoria.

John Jacob Astor became rich by fur trading in the Great Lakes region during the first decade of the 1800s. In 1810, he became a major competitor to the fur companies in Oregon when he created the Pacific Fur Company and an outpost in Astoria.

John Jacob Astor established Fort Astoria, the first permanent settlement in Oregon. Located at the mouth of the Columbia River, Astoria (seen here in a picture from 1849) soon became an important outpost for fur traders.

Left: Men working for the Hudson's Bay Company prepare for a trapping expedition.

Right: The artist Frederic Remington painted this picture of a mountain man, or trapper.

Ashley and Henry

The number of animals that could be trapped back East got very small. As a result, the fur trade went through a slow period. In 1822, a newspaper **advertisement** sparked interest in fur trading again. William Ashley and Andrew Henry, the men who had written the advertisement, called for "**Enterprising Young Men**" to go west with them. Ashley and Henry offered a new style of doing business. Men like Jedediah Smith and Jim Bridger would hunt in the forests of the Rocky Mountains in the Far West. These men became famous as **mountain men**. They started in small teams. Then they set out alone as independent trappers.

DID YOU KNOW?

Back East, trappers worked in large teams. In the Far West, they trapped and explored alone and only visited forts to sell their pelts or to get supplies.

Rendezvous

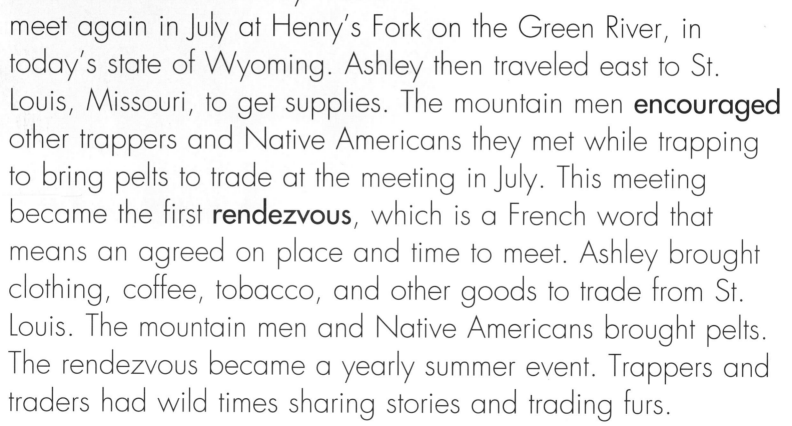

The trappers who worked for William Ashley urged Native Americans, such as those shown here with beaver pelts, to bring the animal skins they trapped to the annual rendezvous for trading.

In the spring of 1825, William Ashley instructed a small hunting party to split up and hunt alone. He said that they would meet again in July at Henry's Fork on the Green River, in today's state of Wyoming. Ashley then traveled east to St. Louis, Missouri, to get supplies. The mountain men **encouraged** other trappers and Native Americans they met while trapping to bring pelts to trade at the meeting in July. This meeting became the first **rendezvous**, which is a French word that means an agreed on place and time to meet. Ashley brought clothing, coffee, tobacco, and other goods to trade from St. Louis. The mountain men and Native Americans brought pelts. The rendezvous became a yearly summer event. Trappers and traders had wild times sharing stories and trading furs.

In this painting by Frederic Remington, a mountain man meets a Native American to trade.

Left: *In this photograph from about 1860, a city gentleman wears a beaver hat.*

Right: *In the 1800s, beavers were the most desirable and valuable fur-bearing animals to trap. This picture of North American beavers was based on a painting by the famous American painter of birds, John James Audubon.*

Beaver Traps

Trappers used simple but clever traps for beavers, the most prized animals to hunt. Beavers swim quickly and can stay underwater for up to five minutes. The men set their steel traps in shallow streams. The traps had strong jaws. When a beaver touched a pad on the bottom of the trap, its legs got caught in the trap's jaws as they clamped shut. Beavers drowned before they had a chance to escape. A long pole stuck into the riverbed held the trap in place. A twig was dipped in a strong beaver scent and hung over the trap. The scent **attracted** other beavers. The trappers collected more of the scent from each beaver they trapped.

DID YOU KNOW?

Trappers labeled the poles that held each of the traps with their names so the owner could be identified. After trappers skinned the beavers that they caught, they also marked the pelts.

Famous Mountain Men

Mountain men, like Jedediah Smith, became **legends** because of their great discoveries and risky adventures. In 1824, Smith was attacked by a grizzly bear and was almost killed. Only 10 days later, he continued his **exploration** and found the South Pass, a 20-mile- (32-km-) wide gap in the Rocky Mountains in present-day Wyoming. Few people knew it existed before that. Smith believed that settlers could use the South Pass to get their wagons through the Rockies.

Mountain man Jim Bridger also made daring discoveries. In 1824, while hunting in the mountains of Utah, Bridger accepted a challenge. One of the other men in the hunting party dared Bridger to follow the nearby Bear River all the way to its source. He accepted the dare, followed the river, and found the Great Salt Lake in Utah.

Top Right: Mountain man Jim Bridger was probably the first white man to see the Great Salt Lake in Utah. Tasting the lake's salty water, Bridger thought he had reached the Pacific Ocean.
Right: Fur trappers with their bundles of furs try to flee a band of attacking Native Americans.

Left: *This mountain man wears clothing made from deerskin, called buckskin.*
Right: *This American dandy, or someone who has very fine clothes and manners, from the 1820s is dressed in a fur-collared cape and a beaver hat.*

The Mountain Men's Success

From the 1820s to the 1840s, mountain men roamed forests, crossed rivers, and climbed mountains. These successful trappers helped prove that a new country like the United States could take over and succeed in **industries** that once had been led by European countries. Their explorations gave the United States great knowledge about the Far West. The mountain men actually lived in this western wilderness beyond the Mississippi River. While they hunted, they learned about the land. They supplied information that helped people to make **official** maps and to correct old maps. The nation learned about western territories that soon would become states.

19

Killing Wildlife

Although the Rocky Mountain fur trade helped to make many people rich, it had some very bad effects, too. Many beavers once lived in the North American wilderness. By the early 1840s, hardly any were still living. Other animals also became scarce. Before the fur trade became important to North America as a business, Native Americans never wasted animals. When they killed an animal, they made clothing from its fur, ate its meat, and even made tools or jewelry with its bones. Then Native Americans joined in the North American fur trade and became a big part of the business. Many traders claimed that Native Americans brought them more furs to sell than mountain men ever did. The fur trade was so **profitable** that even some Native Americans began to waste wildlife, killing animals only for their fur.

Inset: *Trappers traveled west to hunt fur-bearing animals for pelts, such as these fox pelts.* Bottom: *This deer hide is being stretched, perhaps for use as buckskin in making jackets.*

The Last Rendezvous

As many as 2,000 people attended rendezvous during the early 1830s. Only about 120 people attended the one in 1840. It turned out to be the last rendezvous. Fur-bearing animals were hard to find. A lighter, less expensive material, called silk, also came into fashion. People wanted silk instead of fur.

In just about 20 years, the Rocky Mountain fur trade ended most North American fur trading. Mountain men became famous for setting out alone and taking risks to send furs and information back East. They explored the wilderness of the Far West and discovered routes through and across the Rockies. Some mountain men, like Jim Bridger, became guides after they left the fur trade. They helped thousands of American **emigrants** cross through the wilderness to settle in the United States's new, western territories.

Glossary

advertisement (ad-vur-TYZE-ment) A public notice that tries to sell a product or an idea.

attracted (uh-TRAK-ted) To have caused other people, animals, or things to come near something or someone.

emigrants (EH-mih-grents) People who have left their own country to settle somewhere else.

encouraged (in-KUR-ijd) To have given hope, courage, or confidence to someone.

enterprising (EN-tur-pryz-ing) Willing to do something for opportunity.

exploration (ek-spluh-RAY-shun) Travelling over little-known land.

Far West (FAR WEST) The area of land containing the Rocky Mountains and western territories. At the time of the Rocky Mountain fur trade, this area was not part of the United States and mostly was unmapped.

fur-bearing (FER-behr-ing) Having fur.

industries (IN-dus-trees) Businesses that make products or provide services.

legends (LEH-jendz) People or stories that have become famous or important.

manufactured goods (man-yuh-FAK-cherd GOODZ) Things that are made by machine and usually in large quantities.

mountain men (MOUN-ten MEN) Men who live and work in the mountains, rarely leaving them.

official (uh-FIH-shul) Having proof that something is formal or legal.

profitable (PRAH-fih-tuh-bul) Able to earn money.

rendezvous (RON-day-voo) A French word that means an agreed place and time to meet.

scarce (SKEHRS) Something that is small in amount and hard to find but wanted very much.

territory (TEHR-uh-tohr-ee) Land that is controlled by a person or a group of people.

Index

A
Ashley, William, 11, 12
Astor, John Jacob, 8

B
beavers, 15, 20
Bridger, Jim, 11, 16, 22

C
Clark, William, 7

F
Far West, 7, 11, 19, 22

H
Henry, Andrew, 11

J
Jefferson, President Thomas, 7

L
Lewis, Meriwether, 7

N
Native Americans, 4, 12, 20

O
Ohio River Valley, 4, 8

R
rendezvous, 12, 22

S
Smith, Jedediah, 11, 16

T
trappers, 4, 11, 12, 15, 19

U
United States, 7, 8, 19, 22

W
Wyoming, 12, 16

Web Sites

To learn more about the Rocky Mountain fur trade, check out these Web sites:
www.furtrade.org/index.htm
www.pinedaleonline.com/mmmuseum